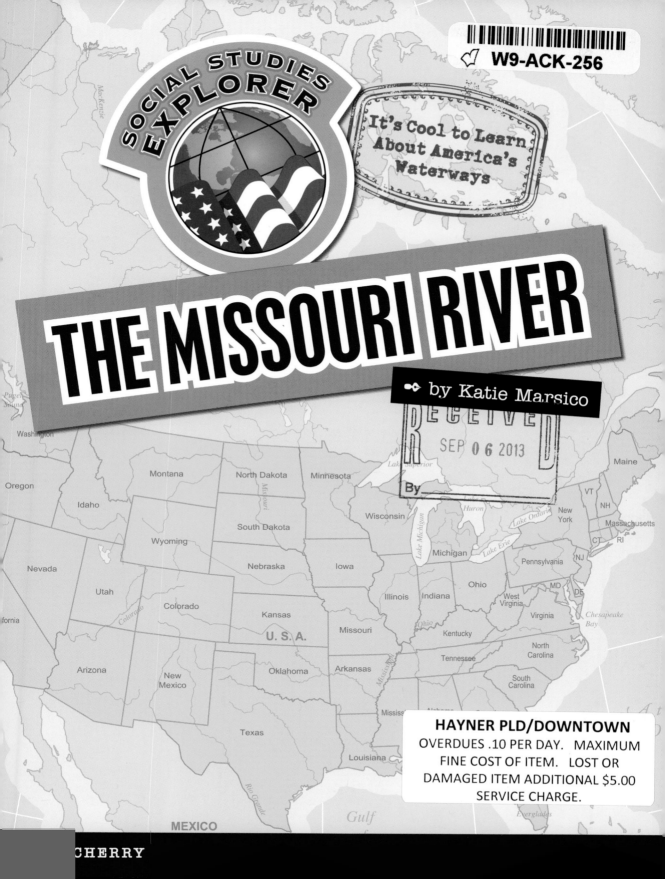

SOCIAL STUDIES EXPLORER

It's Cool to Learn About America's Waterways

THE MISSOURI RIVER

↝ by Katie Marsico

CHERRY

Published in the United States of America
by Cherry Lake Publishing
Ann Arbor, Michigan
www.cherrylakepublishing.com

Content Adviser: James Wolfinger, PhD, Associate Professor,
History and Teacher Education, DePaul University, Chicago, Illinois

Book Design: The Design Lab

Photo Credits: Cover and page 3, ©Tommy Brison/Dreamstime.
com, ©marekuliasz/Shutterstock, Inc., ©Pecold/Shutterstock, Inc.,
©iStockphoto.com/RudyBalasko, ©rook76/Shutterstock, Inc.; back cover
and page 3, ©kavram/Shutterstock, Inc.; page 4, ©Dennis Donohue/
Shutterstock, Inc., page 5, ©trekandshoot/Shutterstock, Inc., page 6,
©welcomia/Shutterstock, Inc., page 8, ©Sue Smith/Shutterstock, Inc.;
page 9, ©Danita Delimont/Alamy; page 10, ©Timothy Lee Lantgen/
Shutterstock, Inc.; page 11, ©Dave Chapman/Alamy; page 12, ©Leslie
McGinnis/Shutterstock, Inc.; page 13, ©Ann Cantelow/Shutterstock, Inc.;
page 15, ©Roger de Montfort/Shutterstock, Inc.; page 16, ©Jason Ross/
Alamy; pages 18 and 19, ©North Wind Picture Archives via AP Images;
page 20, ©Esme/Shutterstock, Inc.; page 22, ©Tom Uhlman/Alamy; page
23, ©Chas/Shutterstock, Inc.; page 26, ©National Geographic Image
Collection/Alamy; page 28, ©kavram/Shutterstock, Inc.

Library of Congress Cataloging-in-Publication Data
Marsico, Katie, 1980–
  The Missouri River / by Katie Marsico.
      p. cm. — (It's cool to learn about America's waterways) (Explorer
library)
  Includes bibliographical references and index.
  ISBN 978-1-62431-010-2 (lib. bdg.) — ISBN 978-1-62431-034-8 (pbk.)
— ISBN 978-1-62431-058-4 (e-book)
1. Missouri River—Description and travel—Juvenile literature. 2. Missouri
River—History—Juvenile literature.
I. Title.
  F598.M26 2013
  978—dc23   2012036821

Cherry Lake Publishing would like to acknowledge the work
of The Partnership for 21st Century Skills. Please visit
www.21stcenturyskills.org for more information.

Printed in the United States of America
Corporate Graphics Inc.
January 2013
CLSP12

THE MISSOURI RIVER

TABLE OF CONTENTS

UNITED STATES POSTAGE 3¢

CHAPTER ONE

WELCOME TO THE MISSOURI RIVER!

➻ The piping plover is one of many bird species you might spot during a trip along the Missouri River.

Are you ready to explore the Missouri River? This water-way is the longest river in North America. Combined with the Mississippi River, it makes up the third-longest river system in the world. During your journey along the Missouri, you'll learn about animals you may have never heard of, such as pallid sturgeons and piping plovers. The first species is a fish and the second is a bird. You'll also have the opportunity to hike past **badlands** and wander across fields filled with tall prairie grass. Before you leave the Missouri River, you'll find out about local American Indian culture. You'll also learn about everything from famous U.S. explorers to steamboats. You'll even get a chance to taste fresh catfish and some of the best barbecue in the country. Most importantly, you'll discover what you can do to help care for an incredible American waterway.

To prepare for your adventure, you'll have to know exactly where you're going. The Missouri River starts in Montana's Rocky Mountains. It stretches 2,500 miles (4,023 kilometers) before emptying into the Mississippi River in Missouri. As it winds first east and then southeast, the Missouri River flows through seven U.S. states. They are Montana, North Dakota, South Dakota, Nebraska, Iowa, Kansas, and Missouri.

Pencils up! Get ready for a few other fast facts about the Missouri River! First, its headwaters (or source) are located 14,000 feet (4,267 meters) above sea level in the Rocky Mountains. As a freshwater mountain stream, it tumbles across the Great Plains, becoming larger and slower moving. The Great Plains is an enormous prairie region that stretches from Canada across the west-central United States.

↝ The Yellowstone River is one of the many waterways that flows into the Missouri.

Of course, if you plan on traveling through the river's entire watershed, you'll have a lot more ground to cover! A watershed, or basin, is the region drained by a river and all of its **tributaries**. The Platte, Kansas, Milk, James, and Yellowstone Rivers are just a few of the 95 major tributaries that flow into the Missouri River.

The Missouri's basin is the largest watershed in the United States. It measures more than 530,000 square miles (1.4 million sq km). The watershed drains one-sixth of the country. It includes portions of all the U.S. states that the river flows through, plus parts of Wyoming, Colorado, Minnesota, and Canada. It will be hard to visit every one of these areas in a single trip. You should probably stay south of the Canadian border on this trip.

ACTIVITY

STOP Don't write in this book!

MISSOURI RIVER MAP

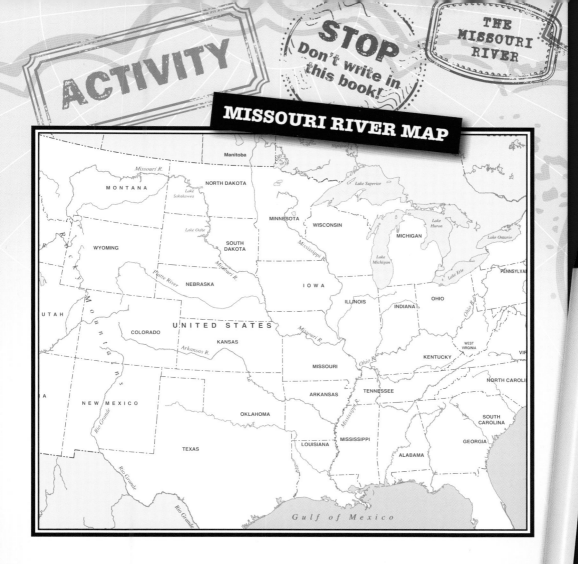

Spend a few minutes looking over this map of the Missouri River. Then lay a separate piece of paper over it and trace the waterway. Mark the Rocky Mountains and the Mississippi River. Also label Montana, North Dakota, South Dakota, Nebraska, Iowa, Kansas, Missouri, Wyoming, Colorado, Minnesota, and Canada. Add any other important locations you read about as you continue your journey along the Missouri River!

Just because you'll soon be exploring a river doesn't mean you are going to spend all of your time in the water! Most of America's waterways—including the Missouri River—support a wide variety of natural **habitats** on nearby land. People often divide the Missouri's watershed into three separate regions to better understand the river's entire **ecosystem**: the Upper Missouri Basin, the Middle Missouri Basin, and the Central Prairie.

The Upper Missouri Basin is made up of land in Montana, Wyoming, South Dakota, North Dakota, and Canada. Much of this area is shrub-steppe. In other words, a large portion of the Upper Missouri watershed is a treeless plain that is covered with low-lying woody plants and wild grasses. You'll also find prairie potholes there. These shallow, sunken marshes formed

➡ The evergreen trees that grow in the Missouri basin in Montana stay green throughout the winter.

Lush forests surround the stretch of the Missouri that flows through Indian Cave State Park in Nebraska.

as a result of the movement of glaciers thousands of years ago. A glacier is a slow-moving mass of ice found in mountain valleys or polar regions.

You'll also run across shrub-steppe and prairie potholes when you arrive in the Middle Missouri Basin. This area stretches through parts of the Dakotas, Colorado, Minnesota, Kansas, Nebraska, Wyoming, and Iowa. Here, you'll also travel through **temperate forests**. Both evergreen and deciduous trees tower above these woodland habitats. Unlike evergreens, deciduous trees shed their leaves every year.

As you pass through the Central Prairie, you'll journey into portions of Missouri and Kansas. Prepare to hike across gently rolling hills and prairies when you visit there. In addition, you'll stroll through oak and hickory forests. These spread across the eastern section of the Central Prairie.

→ Ice and snow often coat the Upper Missouri Basin in winter.

Water temperatures are usually warmer in the lower Missouri River. They sometimes climb higher than 86 degrees Fahrenheit (30 degrees Celsius) in summer months. During winter, however, it is common for portions of the Upper Missouri to freeze over!

Just like water temperature in the river, air temperature in the basin depends on your location and the time of year you are heading there. Pack a heavy coat if you'll tour the headwaters of the Missouri River in winter. Parts of the upper watershed turn as bitterly cold as −60°F (−51°C). If you visit the Middle Missouri and Central Prairie in summer, you can stick to wearing shorts and a tank top. Temperatures there have been known to reach a sizzling 120°F (49°C).

The badlands in the Upper Missouri Basin include dry canyons and flat-topped hills. The climate there is often described as arid. In other words, not much rain falls there. Yet snow is common along the Upper Missouri, especially during harsh winters high in the Rocky Mountains. The Middle Missouri and Central Prairie are slightly more humid than the upper watershed.

Both **droughts** and flooding affect people and wildlife living near the Missouri River. In addition, violent windstorms called tornadoes frequently threaten the Central Prairie during spring and summer months. Don't get too concerned about climate, though! Simply play it safe and check the local weather forecast before you travel.

➝ Tornadoes have caused major damage within the Missouri River's watershed.

CHAPTER TWO

THE WATERWAY'S WILDLIFE

☛ Sagebrush and various types of wild grasses grow in the Upper Missouri watershed.

Are you wondering what else to put in your suitcase before you begin your tour of the Missouri River? It may sound a bit strange, but you should probably pack a magnifying glass. This way, you'll be able to observe even extremely tiny details as you study the amazing wildlife that lives in and along the river!

When you travel through the Upper Missouri watershed, you'll have the opportunity to examine a wide variety of wild grasses. These include grama, needlegrass, and wheatgrass. Shrubs such as sagebrush, rabbitbrush, and yuccas also grow there. Keep your eyes peeled for sunflowers and white prickly poppies!

Do you own a camera? If not, try to borrow one to snap a few photos of the thick clusters of trees in the forests of the Middle Missouri Basin. You'll spot plains cottonwood, green ash, box elder, and American elm throughout these woodland areas.

As you head into the Central Prairie, you might notice the height of the grass. Big bluestem, switchgrass, and Indian grass cover the sloping land. These grasses sometimes grow 7 feet (2.1 m) tall! You'll also glimpse bitternut and shagbark hickories and white, red, and black oaks in the eastern section of the Central Prairie.

Cottonwood trees were named for their white, fluffy seed coverings.

Be sure to bring your binoculars when you explore the Missouri River! You can use them to search the Upper Missouri Basin for prairie dogs, beavers, mule deer, elks, bighorn sheep, coyotes, and mountain lions. Also be on the lookout for gopher snakes, spiny soft-shelled turtles, and tiger **salamanders**. Local bird species range from greater sage grouse and hairy woodpeckers to bald eagles and American white pelicans. By the way, do you remember the pallid sturgeon we mentioned earlier? Well, if you see this fish swimming through the Upper Missouri, don't be shocked by its size. Pallid sturgeons sometimes grow 6 feet (1.8 m) long. They can weigh as much as 80 pounds (36 kilograms)!

Humans affect the health of America's waterways, as well as all the species that depend on them for survival. For example, you won't be able to see several of the animals that once lived in the Upper Missouri. These include grizzly bears, plains bison, and Audubon sheep. Unfortunately, they are no longer found in the region. Overhunting, pollution, and human development of areas in and along the water have wiped them out.

• Woodchucks are also known as groundhogs.

You might notice pallid sturgeons in the Middle Missouri, too. Other fish in the region are shovelnose sturgeon and shortnose gar. This area is also home to pocket gophers, woodchucks, eastern cottontail rabbits, and a variety of other small mammals. The Middle Missouri's bird population includes many different species of hawks, geese, herons, warblers, gulls, grebes, and sparrows.

If you're lucky, perhaps you'll even spy a piping plover! This small bird hunts for insects and tiny **marine** animals in shallow sections of the river. Sadly, piping plovers are threatened. This means they will likely soon face the risk of being wiped off the planet.

◆➡ Spring peepers measure only about an inch (2.5 cm) long.

In the Central Prairie, you'll get a chance to glimpse Canada geese, northern bobwhite quails, and wild turkeys. Local mammals include white-tailed deer, bobcats, coyotes, striped skunks, and gray and red foxes. The Central Prairie is also home to Oklahoma salamanders. You might even spot small frogs called spring peepers.

Fish such as striped shiners, Ozark cavefish, and flathead catfish live in this final stretch of the Missouri River. So do prairie crayfish. However, you may need to use your magnifying glass to get a better look at them. These tiny lobsterlike animals measure only 2 to 3 inches (5.1 to 7.6 centimeters) long. If you want to see prairie crayfish and all the other wildlife in the Missouri River's ecosystem, there's no time to waste. Zip your suitcase, hit the road, and prepare to explore an incredible American waterway!

Make Your Very Own Field Guide

It's important to stay organized as you study the many plants and animals that make up the Missouri River's ecosystem. A field guide is a great way to keep track of all the wildlife you're about to see! Fortunately, you don't need to buy a field guide to explore the Missouri River. You can create your own! First, pick 20 local species (or more if you want). Write the name of each one on a separate sheet of paper. Then prepare to do some detective work on the computer or at the library. Track down and record the following information for the plants and animals you have selected:

Type of plant/animal: (tree, shrub,
    flower/ reptile, mammal, or fish)
Habitat:
Appearance:
Other interesting facts:

After you're done, either print out pictures of the plants and animals or draw them in your field guide. Finally, decorate a cover and staple your pages together. You can also snap them into a binder. Remember to bring your field guide along when you tour the Missouri River!

CHAPTER THREE

PAST AND PRESENT

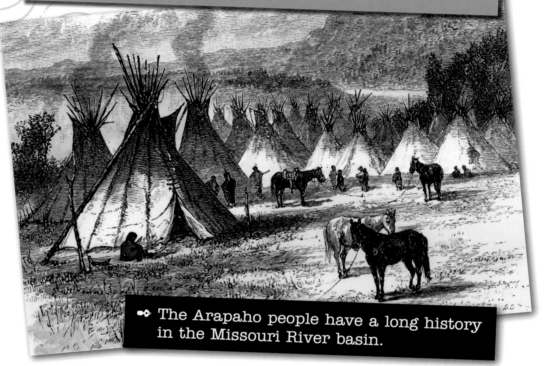

➥ The Arapaho people have a long history in the Missouri River basin.

Close your eyes and imagine that you're not heading to the Missouri River basin today—you're going back 115,000 years in time. That's when the Missouri River started flowing along its present-day course. The river's course changed over tens of millions of years as mountains rose and glaciers moved.

Early peoples probably arrived in the Missouri River basin more than 12,000 years ago. As time passed, many American Indian groups built villages in the Missouri's watershed. Modern American Indian nations in the region include the Arapaho, Blackfoot, Chippewa Cree, Cheyenne, Kickapoo, Mandan, Potawatomi, Sac and Fox, Shoshone, and several branches of Sioux.

Europeans first discovered the Missouri River in the late 1600s. During the next few centuries, the French, British, and Spanish explored the waterway. The rich variety of wildlife drew hunters, trappers, and fur traders.

In the early 1800s, the United States gained control of the Missouri River. Pioneers traveled the waterway as they headed west. Settlers soon developed farms, businesses, and communities throughout much of its basin. Today, this area is home to roughly 10 million people.

➻ French explorers were among the first Europeans to journey along the Missouri River.

Farming is an important part of the **economy** in the Missouri River's watershed. During your travels, you might notice fields filled with corn, soybeans, hay, potatoes, beets, wheat, and cattle. Tourism and **recreational** activities are also big businesses. Major cities on the river include Bismarck, North Dakota; Omaha, Nebraska; and Kansas City, Missouri.

Think about kicking off your journey with a little outdoor adventure at the Missouri National Recreational River. This park is in Nebraska and South Dakota. Visitors enjoy bird-watching, camping, and canoeing. Or you might prefer to hike near the basin's badlands. If so, head to the Upper Missouri River Breaks National Monument in Montana.

Omaha, Nebraska, has a population of roughly 420,000 people.

ACTIVITY

TEST YOUR KNOWLEDGE

So, you think you know about the history of the Missouri River? Test your knowledge with the quick quiz below! On the left side, you'll see the names of five people who are connected to the waterway. On the right side, you'll see a description of the reasons these men and women are famous. Try to match each person with the correct description!

1) Louis Jolliet

A) Shoshone woman who helped guide early U.S. explorers traveling along the Missouri River

2) Meriwether Lewis

B) French explorer who, with Jacques Marquette, was one of the first Europeans to see the Missouri River

3) Sacagawea

C) Sioux leader who led attacks against U.S. settlers throughout the Missouri River basin and who resisted the government's treatment of American Indians

4) Sitting Bull

D) Politician from the Missouri River basin who became the first female governor in the United States

5) Nellie Tayloe Ross

E) U.S. explorer and soldier who, with William Clark, journeyed along the Missouri River and provided detailed descriptions of the waterway's geography, wildlife, and people

Answers: 1) B; 2) E; 3) A; 4) C; 5) D

While you're visiting the Missouri River, don't be afraid to get your feet wet—or muddy! People have nicknamed this waterway the Big Muddy because it carries an extremely large amount of silt. Silt is made up of tiny pieces of sand, clay, mud, and rock.

Would you like to dig deeper into the exciting history of the Missouri River? Simply hop aboard a steamboat called the *Captain Meriwether Lewis* in Brownville, Nebraska. During the 19th and 20th centuries, people depended on steamboats for personal travel and to ship goods along the river. Today, the *Captain Meriwether Lewis* serves as the home of the Museum of Missouri River History. Stop by and discover the amazing stories of local American Indians, early explorers, and bold pioneers!

If you decide you like the view from the water, book a riverboat cruise out of Saint Louis, Missouri. You can journey to the mouth of the Missouri, which is the spot where it meets the Mississippi River. The Central Prairie is also a great place to dig into some traditional Missouri River **cuisine**. Do you enjoy cookouts? Barbecue is especially popular in the Missouri River basin. Different areas within the watershed use different seasonings to spice up pork and other meat cooked over an open fire.

Fresh fish is featured on many menus in the Missouri River basin, as well. Before your trip comes to an end, consider trying catfish! Decide ahead of time whether you want it grilled, blackened, or fried. After you finish your meal, prepare to think about a few serious issues affecting the waterway you've just explored.

There are many ways to serve catfish, including on sandwich bread!

You could pour sauce straight from a bottle. But why not whip up all the fresh flavors of a Kansas City barbecue yourself? Remember that people in different regions in the Missouri River watershed often rely on a specific blend of ingredients to spice up grilled meat. Barbecues in Kansas City frequently feature sauce made from sweet tomatoes, herbs, and mustard. Of course, you don't need to live along the river to sample the tasty recipe below. Make sure to have an adult help you operate the stove at home!

Kansas City-Style Barbecue Sauce

INGREDIENTS

- 2 cups Ketchup
- ⅓ cup dark brown sugar
- 1 tablespoon onion salt
- 1 teaspoon celery salt
- 2 teaspoons garlic powder
- 1 teaspoon chili powder
- 1 teaspoon freshly ground black pepper
- 1 ½ teaspoons ground cumin
- ½ teaspoon ground red pepper
- ¼ cup white vinegar
- 2 tablespoons mustard
- 1 tablespoon lemon juice
- 4 tablespoons butter

INSTRUCTIONS

1. Mix together all of the ingredients except the butter in a medium-size saucepan.

2. Turn on the stovetop and warm the sauce until it simmers, or slowly boils. Stir it over a low heat for the next 30 minutes.

3. Shortly before you turn off the heat, add the butter to the pan. Mix it into your sauce well and then allow everything to cool for a few minutes. Refrigerate the sauce to use later, or drizzle it piping hot over barbecued chicken, beef, or pork. Either way, enjoy a tangy taste of Missouri River cuisine!

CHAPTER FOUR

TAKING CARE OF A NATIONAL TREASURE

➡ Human activity near the Missouri River sometimes leads to pollution of the waterway.

People rely on the Missouri River for everything from recreation to drinking water. Yet their relationship with the river has come at a high price.

Chemicals from nearby farms and factories have leaked into the basin's soil and have polluted the water. Overhunting and overfishing have harmed local wildlife. As a result, certain plant and animal species may disappear completely!

ACTIVITY

GRAPHING WILDLIFE ALONG THE MISSOURI RIVER

The Missouri River supports many more animals than you've read about so far! Experts recently studied about 560 species found along the Missouri River. They determined that roughly 53 percent were birds and 11 percent were mammals. Scientists also estimated that 9 percent of the species they observed were either reptiles or **amphibians**. Approximately 27 percent were fish. Use this information to create a bar graph showing the range of wildlife that relies on healthy Missouri River habitats. Are you able to predict which bar will be the longest? Which do you think will be the shortest?

STOP Don't write in this book!

Many Americans are working hard to rescue these species and to take better care of the Missouri River. U.S. citizens ranging from scientists and government officials to average kids just like you play an important part in **conservation** efforts. For starters, people are trying to find new ways to improve farm and factory processes to eliminate water pollution.

You can help save the Missouri, too! Share everything you have experienced during your adventure. Talk to your friends and family about the plants and animals you have seen and the cultures you have explored. Let them know why the Missouri River deserves to be respected and protected for centuries to come.

Will you help preserve the natural beauty of the Missouri River?

ACTIVITY

WRITE A LETTER

Politicians in Montana, North Dakota, South Dakota, Nebraska, Iowa, Kansas, Missouri, Wyoming, Colorado, and Minnesota are able to influence the future of the Missouri River. Together with other government officials across America, they vote on issues and plan projects that affect U.S. waterways. Writing a letter to these individuals makes them aware that people like you care about the Missouri River. Ask an adult to help you find the addresses of political leaders who support conservation efforts in and along the river. Then create a short, simple letter using the following outline:

Dear [INSERT THE NAME OF THE POLITICIAN(S) YOU DECIDE TO WRITE TO]:

I am writing to ask for your help in protecting the Missouri River. The river is important to me because [INSERT TWO OR THREE REASONS THE RIVER MATTERS TO YOU].

Thanks for your efforts to support this amazing American waterway!

Sincerely,

[INSERT YOUR NAME]

STOP
Don't write in this book!

GLOSSARY

amphibians (am-FIB-ee-uhnz) cold-blooded animals with a backbone that live in water and breathe with gills when young; as adults, they develop lungs and live on land

badlands (BAD-landz) areas of barren land with rough ridges and peaks

conservation (kahn-sur-VAY-shuhn) the protection of valuable things, especially wildlife, natural resources, forests, or artistic or historic objects

cuisine (kwi-ZEEN) a style or manner of cooking or presenting food

droughts (DROUTZ) long periods without rain

economy (i-KAH-nuh-mee) the system of buying, selling, making things, and managing money in a place

ecosystem (EE-koh-sis-tuhm) all the livings things in a place and their relation to the environment

habitats (HAB-uh-tats) places where an animal or a plant naturally lives

marine (muh-REEN) of or having to do with the ocean

recreational (rek-ree-AY-shuhn-uhl) involving games, sports, and hobbies that people like to do in their spare time

salamanders (SAL-uh-man-durz) animals that look like small, brightly colored lizards

temperate forests (TEM-pur-it FOR-ists) woodlands with a mild climate and leaf-shedding trees

tributaries (TRIB-yu-ter-eez) streams that flow into a larger stream, river, or lake

BOOKS

Domnauer, Teresa. *The Lewis and Clark Expedition*. New York: Children's Press, 2012.

Murray, Julie. *Missouri*. Minneapolis: ABDO Publishing Company, 2013.

WEB SITES

**Missouri Department of Natural Resources—
Lewis and Clark Water Trail**
http://dnr.mo.gov/water-trail/riverhistory.htm
This site offers information about the Missouri River, from facts describing historic steamboat traffic to current data.

**National Park Service (NPS)—
Missouri National Recreational River: For Kids**
www.nps.gov/mnrr/forkids/index.htm
This site features online puzzles and word searches that focus on the Missouri River, as well as information on becoming a junior ranger in the NPS.

INDEX

ABOUT THE AUTHOR
Katie Marsico has written more than 100 books for young readers. She hopes to eventually tour the Missouri River with her own band of explorers— Carl, Maria, C. J., Thomas, and Megan.